A *Doonesbury* book

# Do All Birders Have Bedroom Eyes, Dear?

D1024101

## G.B. Trudeau

Selected Cartoons from
*ASK FOR MAY, SETTLE FOR JUNE* Vol. 2

FAWCETT CREST • NEW YORK

A Fawcett Crest Book
Published by Ballantine Books
Copyright © 1981, 1982 by G. B. Trudeau

Library of Congress Catalog Card Number: 81-84328

ISBN 0-449-20194-5

This edition published by arrangement with Holt, Rinehart
and Winston

Selected cartoons from ASK FOR MAY,
SETTLE FOR JUNE Vol. 2

The cartoons in this book have appeared in newspapers in the United States and abroad under the auspices of Universal Press Syndicate.

Manufactured in the United States of America

First Ballantine Books Edition: July 1983

10  9  8  7  6  5  4  3  2  1

# Do All Birders Have Bedroom Eyes, Dear?

Joan Caucus
and Bick Redfern
invite you to their
wedding at 3:00 p.m.
at 312 Foxhunt Rd.
Washington, D.C.

R.S.V.P.

"BICK"? WHO'S THIS "BICK"? AND WHERE'S THE DATE?

MAYBE THIS LITTLE SLIP EXPLAINS IT..

YOU CAN'T KEEP ANYTHING FROM NEIGHBORS, DEAR. THEY ALWAYS FIND OUT. THEY EVEN FOUND OUT RICK IS A.. A REPORTER!

SO?

WELL, YOU KNOW HOW PEOPLE MIS-TRUST THE MEDIA THESE DAYS..

YOU'RE TELLING ME. I HAVE TO PAY CASH FOR EVERYTHING.

GB Trudeau

GOOD EVENING. TODAY THE STATE DEPARTMENT FINALLY CONCEDED THAT ITS HIGHLY ACCLAIMED "WHITE PAPER" ON SOVIET INTERFERENCE IN EL SALVADOR WAS RIDDLED WITH ERRORS AND MISLEADING STATEMENTS.

THE WHITE PAPER, SUBTITLED "SHAFIK: PORTRAIT OF A COMMUNIST," HAD BEEN WIDELY USED BY OFFICIALS TO DEFEND U.S. MILITARY AID TO THE REPRESSIVE REGIME OF JOSÉ DUARTE.

TODAY, SECRETARY OF STATE HAIG ACCEPTED FULL RESPONSIBILITY FOR THE FRAUDULENT REPORT, ADMITTING THAT HE AND OTHER TRUSTING OFFICIALS HAD BEEN DUPED BY THE REPORT'S YOUNG AUTHOR, JON D. GLASSMAN.

SAID A SHAKEN HAIG, "DISGRACE-WISE, THIS IS A DIRECT HIT."

OF COURSE, "SHAFIK" EXISTS. IT'S JUST THAT THE EVIDENCE OF HIS ACTIVITIES IS INCONCLUSIVE. BUT IF "SHAFIK" DIDN'T INVITE SOVIET INTERFERENCE IN EL SALVADOR, THEN OTHERS JUST LIKE HIM DID.

THEN "SHAFIK" IS, IN EFFECT, A COMPOSITE COMMUNIST?

RIGHT. I JUST DIDN'T WANT TO BREAK UP THE FLOW OF THE STORY.

WHY DIDN'T THE STATE DEPARTMENT CATCH THE GLARING ERRORS AND FABRICATIONS OF THE EL SALVADOR "WHITE PAPER"? FOGGY BOTTOM TOPSIDER ED FROST EXPLAINS..

LOOK, WHEN I FIRST READ "SHAFIK: PORTRAIT OF A COMMUNIST," I WAS SKEPTICAL MYSELF. IT SEEMED TOO PAT. BUT THE WRITER WAS ONE OF OUR STAR BUREAUCRATS. WE TRUSTED HIM.

SECRETARY HAIG, DID YOU REVIEW THE EL SALVADOR "WHITE PAPER" BEFORE IT WAS PUBLISHED?

AFFIRMATIVE. EXTENUATINGLY, MY INPUT WAS RESTRICTED TO SYNTAX AND GRAMMAR. I TRUSTED THE WRITER IMPLICITLY, AND HAD NO FOREWARNING HE WAS PREDISPOSED TO DISGRACING HIS UNIFORM.

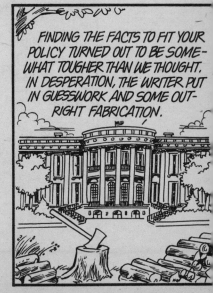